ABUNDANT TRUTH INTERNATIONAL MINISTRIES

Abundant Truth International's Inspirational Series

KEYS TO THE PROMISES OF GOD

Maintaining Faith While You Wait

Roderick Levi Evans

Keys to the Promises of God
Maintaining Faith While You Wait

All Rights Reserved © 2024 by Roderick L. Evans

No part of this book may be reproduced or transmitted in any form or by any means, graphic, electronic, or mechanical, including photocopying, recording, taping, or by any information storage or retrieval system, without the permission in writing from the publisher.

Front & Back Cover Designs by Abundant Truth Publishing

Abundant Truth Publishing
an imprint of Abundant Truth International Ministries

For information address:
Abundant Truth International
P.O. Box 126
Camden, NC 27921

Unless otherwise indicated all of the scripture quotations are taken from the Authorized King James Version of the Bible. Scripture quotations marked with NIV are taken from the New International Version of the Bible. Scriptures marked with NASV are taken for the New American Standard Version of the Bible.

ISBN 13: 978-1601415752

Printed in the United States of America.

CONTENTS

Introduction

Chapter 1: The Promise is Made — 1

Forsaking the World — 6

Ignoring the Circumstances — 7

Chapter 2: The Promise is Delayed — 13

It's Not Your Fault — 15

It's God's Plan — 17

Chapter 3: The Promise is Clarified — 23

Change Self-Perception — 27

CONTENTS (cont.)

Change Approach to God · · · · · 31

Chapter 4: The Promise is Fulfilled · · · · · 37

God Keeps His Promise · · · · · 41

Chapter 5: Your "Sarah" will have a Son · · · · · 45

Wait on the Appointed Time · · · · · 49

Wait in Faith · · · · · 51

Bibliography · · · · · 55

Scripture References · · · · · 59

The Promise of an Heir · · · · · 61

CONTENTS (cont.)

Abraham and Sarah is Promised a Son   63

Introduction

The Christian life is simple and complex simultaneously. Its simplicity rests upon one truth: Jesus Christ is the Son of God and that faith in Him results in man's salvation. However, to live a fruitful Christian life comes from navigating through the complexities of life.

The Abundant Truth Inspirational Series was developed to aid the Christian in handling the difficulties that come with the Christian experience.

In this Publication

Do you keep promises that you make? How many times in life have we been disappointed because someone made us a promise and did not keep it?

We know that God is not like man. Whatever He says He is going to do, it shall be done. Whatever He has promised in the scriptures will surely be manifested in your life.

In light of this truth, many still have felt as if the Lord had forgotten them and begun to doubt the promises that He made to them. However, the Lord is going to perform His word.

In the biblical account of the patriarch Abraham, we find that God made him a promise. He told Abraham that he would have a son. However, he had to wait.

After some time had passed, Sarah did not conceive, and Abraham fathered a son by his handmaiden, Hagar. However, we discover that this was not the child of promise.

After more years had passed, we discover that God performed His word to Abraham and Sarah did have a son. From this story, we shall explore some valuable truths that will help us stand as we **wait** to possess the promise.

In the publication, we will look closely at the biblical account of God's promise to Abraham. From this, will discover truth to help Christians today to maintain faith as we wait on the promises of God.

KEYS TO THE PROMISES

Maintaining Faith While You Wait

-Chapter 1-

The Promise is Made

KEYS TO THE PROMISES
Maintaining Faith While You Wait

And, behold, the word of the Lord came unto him, saying, This shall not be thine heir; but he that shall come forth out of thine own bowels shall be thine heir. (Genesis 15:4)

KEYS TO THE PROMISES

Maintaining Faith While You Wait

After Abram (Abraham) returns from battle and gives tithes to Melchizedek, the Lord appears to him in a vision.

After these things the word of the Lord came unto Abram in a vision, saying, Fear not, Abram: I am thy shield, and thy exceeding great reward. And Abram said, Lord God, what wilt thou give me, seeing I go childless, and the steward of my house is this Eliezer of Damascus? And Abram said, Behold, to me thou hast given no seed: and, lo, one born in my house is mine heir. (Genesis 15:1-3)

Abram asks the Lord that if you are my shield and exceeding great reward, then why have I not had a son.

Forsaking the World

Abram had left everything familiar to him to follow the Lord. However, the Lord did not bless him with a child. Does his question to the Lord sound like us today?

We have left the world and the lusts therein only to find that we have not received all that we think the Lord should give us. This was the mindset of Abram. Following in the passage, we find that God speaks to Abram and tells him that he would have the son that he has desired.

> *And, behold, the word of the Lord came unto him, saying, This shall not be thine heir; but he that shall come forth out of thine own bowels shall be thine heir. (Genesis 15:4)*

Ignoring the Circumstances

God spoke this to him in spite of the facts:

1. *He was old.*

2. *Sarai, his wife, was old.*

3. *Sarai was barren.*

We discover, in spite of the obstacles, that Abram believed the Lord.

And he believed in the Lord; and he counted it to him for righteousness. (Genesis 15:6)

We, too, must stand on the promises of God. God made him a promise in the most unfavorable conditions. We must understand that our present circumstances and conditions do not negate or hinder the promises of God from coming to pass in our lives.

If God has made you a promise or you are believing God for something by faith – continue to believe. If Abram could believe against the odds, so can we.

Personal Thoughts:

_____

_____

_____

_____

_____

_____

_____

_____

KEYS TO THE PROMISES
Maintaining Faith While You Wait

_____

_____

_____

_____

_____

_____

_____

_____

_____

-Chapter 2-

The Promise is Delayed

When we think of the something being delayed, it is often attributed to some outside influence. However, the plan of God cannot be delayed except by God himself.

It's Not Your Fault

Do not think that you have done something wrong or someone else is hindering your blessing or promise from coming to pass. Whatever the Lord has for you, it is for you.

In our story, God did not bring the promise to pass immediately. We find that because of this, Sarai tells Abram to take her handmaid and have an heir by her.

And Sarai said unto Abram, Behold now, the Lord hath restrained me from bearing: I pray thee, go in unto my maid; it may be that I may obtain children by her. And Abram hearkened to the voice of Sarai. (Genesis 16:2)

This was **not** because they did not believe God.

He staggered not at the promise of God through unbelief; but was strong in faith, giving glory to God. (Romans 4:20)

It's God's Plan

For in God's promise to Abram, He had made no mention of Sarai. He told Abram from **his** own bowels would an heir come. Since the customs of the day allowed such a practice, Abram went into Hagar and she conceived and brought forth a son, calling him Ishmael.

And Hagar bare Abram a son: and Abram called his son's name, which Hagar bare, Ishmael. (Genesis 16: 15)

However, we discover that this was not the fulfillment of the promise. How many times did it seem you were close to walking in what the Lord had promised, only to discover that it was not His will?

Oftentimes, we like Abram, produce "Ishmael" in our lives and we think it is the promise. This is why many are disappointed and discouraged.

When they thought God's promise was coming to pass and it was not received, rather than standing on the promise, they began to doubt that God had ever spoken to them.

We cannot doubt God's promise

because of apparent delays and setbacks.

His word to us will come to pass.

KEYS TO THE PROMISES
Maintaining Faith While You Wait

Personal Thoughts:

_____

_____

_____

_____

_____

_____

_____

_____

KEYS TO THE PROMISES
Maintaining Faith While You Wait

_____

_____

_____

_____

_____

_____

_____

_____

_____

-Chapter 3-

The Promise is Clarified

KEYS TO THE PROMISES
Maintaining Faith While You Wait

And when Abram was ninety years old and nine, the Lord appeared to Abram, and said unto him, I am the Almighty God; walk before me, and be thou perfect. (Genesis 17:1)

KEYS TO THE PROMISES
Maintaining Faith While You Wait

Abram thought he was on his way. Hagar gave him a son who would be his heir. However, the Lord appears to him almost 13 years after the initial promise and gives Abram clarity.

> *And when Abram was ninety years old and nine, the Lord appeared to Abram, and said unto him, I am the Almighty God; walk before me, and be thou perfect. (Genesis 17:1)*

Change Self-Perception

The first thing God does is change his name to Abraham and give him the sign of circumcision.

Neither shall thy name any more be called Abram, but thy name shall be Abraham; for a father of many nations have I made thee. (Genesis 17:5)

Next, God tells Abraham to change his wife's name. In addition, God brings further clarity to the word originally spoken to Abraham. He would have a son, but it would be by his barren and old wife. Abraham was shocked and he laughed.

And God said unto Abraham, As for Sarai thy wife, thou shalt not call her name Sarai, but Sarah shall her name be. And I will bless her, and give thee a son also of her: yea, I will bless her, and she shall be a mother of nations; kings of people shall be of her. (Genesis 17:1516)

He even pleaded with the Lord for Ishmael. He wanted him to be his heir. However, the Lord would not hear it.

Then Abraham fell upon his face, and laughed, and said in his heart, Shall a child be born unto him that is an hundred years old? and shall Sarah, that is ninety years old, bear? And Abraham said unto God, O that

Ishmael might live before thee! And God said, Sarah thy wife shall bear thee a son indeed; and thou shalt call his name Isaac: and I will establish my covenant with him for an everlasting covenant, and with his seed after him. (Genesis 17:17-19)

This is where many believers miss the Lord. We, like Abraham, did not go back to the Lord with follow up questions after the promise is made.

This is the reason many people suffer unnecessary setbacks as they move toward the promises of God. They did not get clarity in the promise.

Change Approach to God

Since God had made mention Only of Abraham years earlier, Abraham did not ask God by whom he would have a child. We can suggest that he assumed it would be by someone other than his wife.

Because he asked no questions, he had to now deal with the fact that the son (from Hagar) whom he thought would be his heir was rejected by God.

In addition, he had to stand in faith

again as God now mentioned his heir coming from his old, barren wife. Paul tells us that after his dialogue with the Lord, he believed the Lord for it by faith.

And being not weak in faith, he considered not his own body now dead, when he was about an hundred years old, neither yet the deadness of Sarah's womb. (Romans 4:19)

Some of you reading this have left off believing God for His promises because of delays and setbacks. It is time now for you to return to the Lord and ask for clarity regarding His promise. Some of your efforts have been fruitless because you have been going in unto Hagar and not Sarah.

KEYS TO THE PROMISES
Maintaining Faith While You Wait

KEYS TO THE PROMISES
Maintaining Faith While You Wait

Personal Thoughts:

_____

_____

_____

_____

_____

_____

_____

KEYS TO THE PROMISES
Maintaining Faith While You Wait

-Chapter 4-

The Promise is Fulfilled

KEYS TO THE PROMISES
Maintaining Faith While You Wait

And Abraham called the name of his son that was born unto him, whom Sarah bare to him, Isaac.

KEYS TO THE PROMISES
Maintaining Faith While You Wait

God fulfills His promise to Abraham. Sarah conceives and brings forth Isaac.

> *And the Lord visited Sarah as he had said, and the Lord did unto Sarah as he had spoken. For Sarah conceived, and bare Abraham a son in his old age, at the set time of which God had spoken to him. And Abraham called the name of his son that was born unto him, whom Sarah bare to him, Isaac. (Genesis 21:1-3)*

God Keeps His Promise

The word of the Lord came to pass in

a way that Abraham and Sarah did not think it would. In addition, the son was called Isaac, meaning "laughter."

This demonstrates to us that when God brings forth his promise in your life, you will have joy and laughter.

Personal Thoughts:

_____

_____

_____

_____

_____

_____

_____

_____

KEYS TO THE PROMISES
Maintaining Faith While You Wait

_____

_____

_____

_____

_____

_____

_____

_____

_____

-Chapter 5-

Your "Sarah" will have a Son

KEYS TO THE PROMISES
Maintaining Faith While You Wait

God wants you to try again. After the Lord made his promise plain to Abraham, the only thing he had to do was to go in unto Sarah again.

KEYS TO THE PROMISES
Maintaining Faith While You Wait

Many of you have tried to wait and walk in the promise and plan of God your lives without major results. Therefore, (like Abraham going into Hagar), your attention was still on the promise, but diverted to areas that seemed to be more productive.

Abraham did not realize that the woman he had gone into for years, without producing any fruit would be the one that would give him an heir.

Wait on the Appointed Time

This demonstrates to us that God's promise to us is always with us, just waiting until the appointed time to produce fruit. The very one that never gave him a son, became the vessel of his promise.

This shows us that the areas in our lives and ministries that have not been very productive will bring forth fruit, if we turn our attention from "Hagar and Ishmael" and focus again on "Sarah."

God wants you to try again. After the Lord made his promise plain to Abraham, the only thing he had to do was to go in unto Sarah again.

Wait in Faith

Many have given up on their ministries growing, family members receiving salvation, and even their bodies being healed. They have prayed, fasted, claimed, and believed and no results were found. However, walk in the faith of Abraham and go in again unto "Sarah."

Believe God again for growth in your ministry, present the gospel again unto unsaved family members, pray and believe God again for your healing.

For whatever your "Sarah" is, she will conceive and bring forth your "Isaac." This is the reward of the Art of Waiting.

Personal Thoughts:

_____

_____

_____

_____

_____

_____

_____

_____

KEYS TO THE PROMISES
Maintaining Faith While You Wait

Bibliography

Smith, William. *Smith's Bible Dictionary.* Holman Bible Publishers. Nashville, Tennessee. c1994

The Bible Library. *The Bible Library CD Rom Disc.* Ellis Enterprises Incorporated, (c)1988 – 2000. 4205 McAuley Blvd., Suite 385, Oklahoma City, OK 73120. All Rights Reserved.

Lockman Foundation. *Comparative Study Bible.* Zondervan Publishing House. Grand Rapids, MI, c1984

Personal Thoughts:

_____

_____

_____

_____

_____

_____

_____

KEYS TO THE PROMISES
Maintaining Faith While You Wait

-Appendix-

Scripture References

The Promise of an Heir
Genesis 15:1-7

1After these things the word of the LORD came unto Abram in a vision, saying, Fear not, Abram: I am thy shield, and thy exceeding great reward.

2And Abram said, Lord GOD, what wilt thou give me, seeing I go childless, and the steward of my house is this Eliezer of Damascus?

3And Abram said, Behold, to me thou hast given no seed: and, lo, one born in my house is mine heir.

4And, behold, the word of the LORD came

unto him, saying, This shall not be thine heir; but he that shall come forth out of thine own bowels shall be thine heir.

5And he brought him forth abroad, and said, Look now toward heaven, and tell the stars, if thou be able to number them: and he said unto him, So shall thy seed be.

6And he believed in the LORD; and he counted it to him for righteousness.

7And he said unto him, I am the LORD that brought thee out of Ur of the Chaldees, to give thee this land to inherit it.

Abraham Is Promised a Son
Genesis 18:1-18

1 The Lord showed Himself to Abraham by the oak trees of Mamre, as he sat at the tent door in the heat of the day. 2 Abraham looked up and saw three men standing in front of him. When he saw them, he ran from the tent door to meet them. He put his face to the ground 3 and said, "My lord, if I have found favor in your eyes, please do not pass by your servant. 4

Let us have a little water brought to wash your feet. Rest yourselves under the tree. 5 And I will get a piece of bread so you may eat and get strength. After that you may go on your way, since you have come to your servant."

The men said, "Do as you have said." 6 So Abraham ran into the tent to Sarah, and said, "Hurry and get three pails of fine flour, mix it well, and make bread." 7 Then Abraham ran to the cattle and took out a young and good calf. He gave it to the servant to make it ready in a hurry. 8 He took milk and cheese and the meat which he had made ready, and set it in front of them. He stood by them under the tree while they ate.

9 Then they said to him, "Where is your wife Sarah?" And he said, "There in the tent." 10 The Lord said, "I will be sure to return to you at this time next year. And your wife Sarah will have a son." Sarah was listening at the tent door behind him. 11 Now Abraham

and Sarah were old. They had lived many years. The way of women had stopped for Sarah. 12 So Sarah laughed to herself, saying, "Will I have this joy after my husband and I have grown old?" 13 Then the Lord said to Abraham, "Why did Sarah laugh and say, 'How can I give birth to a child when I am so old?' 14 Is anything too hard for the Lord? I will return to you at this time next year, and Sarah will have a son." 15 But Sarah said, "I did not laugh," because she was afraid.

And He said, "No, but you did laugh."

KEYS TO THE PROMISES
Maintaining Faith While You Wait

Personal Thoughts:

_____

_____

_____

_____

_____

_____

_____

_____

KEYS TO THE PROMISES
Maintaining Faith While You Wait

Unless otherwise indicated all of the scripture quotations are taken from the Authorized King James Version of the Bible. Scripture quotations marked with NIV are taken from the New International Version of the Bible. Scriptures marked with NASV are taken for the New American Standard Version of the Bible.

www.ingramcontent.com/pod-product-compliance
Lightning Source LLC
Chambersburg PA
CBHW050343010526
44119CB00049B/678